Too Many Signs!

Keep Off Grass

by E.J. Nikki
illustrated by Gillian Roberts

 HOUGHTON MIFFLIN HARCOURT
School Publishers

Printed in China

ISBN-13: 978-0-547-02179-9
ISBN-10: 0-547-02179-8

3 4 5 6 7 8 0940 18 17 16 15 14 13 12 11 10

The mayor of Happytown was an orderly man. "People should follow the rules," he liked to say.

The mayor was happy with his town. When he looked around, he noticed that everything in town was running smoothly. Everyone was getting around safely. Everything looked beautiful.

"I do love a good sign," he liked to say. "Signs tell the rules, and rules keep everyone happy."

But the people in Happytown were not happy. Everyone was tired of following all the signs. There were too many of them. And if they did not follow the signs, the policeman gave them a ticket.

Everyone was always getting tickets.

One day, Ms. Gold was running on the sidewalk.

"Tweet!" The policeman blew his whistle. "Stop running on the sidewalk!"

"But I am just trying to get some exercise," said Ms. Gold.

"The sign says 'No Running'! Here's your ticket!" the policeman said.

Ms. Gold was confused. She got a ticket for exercising? That did not make her happy— not at all.

The next day, Mr. Smith and his dog were caught dancing in front of the music store. There was great music coming from inside. They couldn't help themselves.

"Tweet!" The policeman blew his whistle. "Stop dancing!"

"But officer, sir, we just love this song." Mr. Smith tried to be polite.

"The sign says 'No Dancing'!" the policeman told him. "Here's your ticket!"

Mr. Smith was confused. He just got a ticket for dancing to music? That did not make him happy—not at all.

The day after that, Ms. Perez walked onto the grass to smell the flowers. She especially loved the roses in the center of town.

"Tweet!" The policeman blew his whistle. "Get off the grass!"

"But I am just smelling the flowers," explained Ms. Perez.

"The sign says 'Keep Off the Grass'!" said the policeman. "Here's your ticket!"

Ms. Perez was confused. She got a ticket for enjoying flowers? That did not make her happy— not at all.

Ms. Gold, Mr. Smith and his dog, and Ms. Perez got the townspeople together. They were tired of always getting in <mark>trouble</mark>. They were tired of all the tickets. So they asked the mayor for a meeting.

"We no longer want signs telling us what we can and cannot do. We are smart enough to know what to do."

The townspeople all <mark>agreed</mark> and started shouting, "No More Signs! No More Signs!"

The mayor explained, "But the signs keep order in our town. Without signs, everyone will be unhappy."

"No, we won't be unhappy. We will all be much happier!" they shouted.

The mayor was elected because of his wisdom. He knew that if the town had no signs, the townspeople would live in complete disorder. But he failed to convince them.

So the mayor told his assistant to start tearing down all the signs—every single one.

"Hooray!" the townspeople cheered.

The mayor's assistant **cleared** the streets of all signs. He cleared the buildings of all signs. There was not a sign to be seen anywhere in Happytown.

The townspeople went wild. They could do the opposite of what they were allowed to do before.

Ms. Gold went running on the sidewalk. Soon everyone was running on the sidewalk. They started bumping into one another and falling down, but no tickets were given.

Mr. Smith and his dog danced in front of the
music store. Soon there was a huge crowd dancing
with them. The crowd was so big and they were
dancing so much that no one could get in the door
of the shop to buy the music. But no tickets were
given.

The mayor and the policeman just watched.

Ms. Perez went to smell the flowers. Other people joined her. Many people decided not just to smell the flowers but to pick them, too. Soon the flower beds were completely bare.

Lots of people walked on the grass. They had picnics and barbeques. They played baseball and football. Soon all the grass began to wear away.

People drove wherever they wanted to. They went the wrong way down one-way streets. They drove in the exits of parking lots. They drove out the entrances of parking lots. Everyone got in one another's way, and none of the cars got very far. In fact, some of the cars sat in traffic all day!

"Do you think they have learned their lesson?" the policeman asked the mayor.

"Not yet," the mayor said.

People stopped using the garbage cans for garbage. They threw all their garbage on the ground. Piles of garbage grew high—and highly stinky! What a mess!

"Now they've learned their lesson," said the mayor to the policeman.

"I believe you're right," the policeman said.

Miss Gold, Mr. Smith and his dog, and Ms.
Perez got the townspeople together. They asked
the mayor for a meeting.

"We want our signs back," they told him.

"Are you sure?" asked the mayor.

The townspeople started shouting, "We want
signs! We want signs!"

So the mayor had his assistant put all the signs
back up.

"Hooray!" the townspeople cheered.

What a huge relief it was to have all the signs back! Everyone knew what to do and where to go. Everything looked beautiful again. And best of all, everybody was safe.

"I do love a good sign," the mayor said to the policeman. "Signs tell the rules, and rules keep everyone happy. But you know what?" he told the policeman. "Let's stop giving everyone tickets."

And so they did.

Now everyone was very happy in Happytown.

Responding

✔ **TARGET SKILL** **Text and Graphic Features** How does punctuation help you read this story? Copy and complete the chart below.

Page Numbers	Punctuation	How It Helps
2,3,4,5,6,7,11,12, 13,14 ? ?	Quotation marks ? ?	Shows someone is speaking ? ?

 Write About It

Text to Self Imagine that you and your friends are going to Mars! Write a fictional narrative paragraph about your trip. Remember to introduce the characters and setting, explain the problem, and tell how the problem is solved.

TARGET VOCABULARY

agreed	polite
assistant	tearing
cleared	trouble
failed	wisdom

EXPAND YOUR VOCABULARY

disorder	orderly
opposite	relief

TARGET SKILL **Text and Graphic Features** Tell how words work with art.

TARGET STRATEGY **Question** Ask questions about what you are reading.

GENRE **Humorous fiction** is a story that is written to make the reader laugh.